Contents

Book Title	Crime/Horror	Classic	Romance	Fantasy/Sci-fi	Historical	Biography	[Personal Preference]	[Personal Preference]	[Personal Preference]
1									
2									
3									
4									
5									
6									
7									
8									
9									
10									
11									
12									
13									
14									
15									
16									
17									
18									
19									
20									
21									
22									
23									
24									
25									

Book Title	Crime/Horror	Classic	Romance	Fantasy/Sci-fi	Historical	Biography	[Personal Preference]	[Personal Preference]	[Personal Preference]
26									
27									
28									
29									
30									
31									
32									
33									
34									
35									
36									
37									
38									
39									
40									
41									
42									
43									
44									
45									
46									
47									
48									
49									
50									

Book Title	Crime/Horror	Classic	Romance	Fantasy/Sci-fi	Historical	Biography	[Personal Preference]	[Personal Preference]	[Personal Preference]
51									
52									
53									
54									
55									
56									
57									
58									
59									
60									
61									
62									
63									
64									
65									
66									
67									
68									
69									
70									
71									
72									
73									
74									
75									

Book Title	Crime/Horror	Classic	Romance	Fantasy/Sci-fi	Historical	Biography	[Personal Preference]	[Personal Preference]	[Personal Preference]
76									
77									
78									
79									
80									
81									
82									
83									
84									
85									
86									
87									
88									
89									
90									
91									
92									
93									
94									
95									
96									
97									
98									
99									
100									

Paperback ○   Hardback ○   e-book ○   Audiobook ○

Title:

1

Author: _____

Publisher: _____   Pub. date _____

Page count: _____

○ Fiction   ○ Non-fiction
  Genre: _____   Subject: _____

My Review: _____
_____
_____
_____
_____
_____
_____
_____
_____
_____
_____
_____
_____

Great quotes from this book:

Dates
Started: _____
Finished: _____

Source
Bought ○   Loaned ○
From: _____

Inspiration Tree

Why I read it?
_____
↓
It inspired me to
(read/learn/visit)?
_____
_____
↓
Who will I
recommend it to?
_____

⋇ Ratings ⋇

Plot: 1 2 3 4 5
Characters:
1 2 3 4 5
Ease of reading:
1 2 3 4 5
Overall
☹ 😐 🙂

2

Paperback ○   Hardback ○   e-book ○   Audiobook ○

Title:

Dates
Started: _____
Finished: _____

Source
Bought ○   Loaned ○
From: _____

Author: _____

Publisher: _____   Pub. date _____

Page count: _____

○ Fiction   ○ Non-fiction

Genre: _____   Subject: _____

My Review: _____

_____
_____
_____
_____
_____
_____
_____
_____
_____
_____
_____
_____
_____
_____
_____

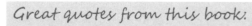

Inspiration Tree

Why I read it?
_____
↓
It inspired me to
(read/learn/visit)?
_____
↓
Who will I
recommend it to?
_____

✸ Ratings ✸

Plot: 1 2 3 4 5
Characters:
1 2 3 4 5
Ease of reading:
1 2 3 4 5
Overall

Great quotes from this book:

Paperback ○   Hardback ○   e-book ○   Audiobook ○

Title:

3

Author: _____

Publisher: _____ Pub. date _____

Page count: _____

○ Fiction   ○ Non-fiction

Genre: _____   Subject: _____

Dates
Started: _____
Finished: _____

Source
Bought ○ Loaned ○
From: _____

My Review: _____

_____

_____

_____

_____

_____

_____

_____

_____

_____

_____

_____

_____

Inspiration Tree

Why I read it?
_____
↓
It inspired me to
(read/learn/visit)?

_____

_____
↓
Who will I
recommend it to?

_____

Great quotes from this book:

✳ Ratings ✳

Plot: 1 2 3 4 5
Characters:
1 2 3 4 5
Ease of reading:
1 2 3 4 5
Overall
☹ 😐 🙂

4

Title:

Dates
Started: _____
Finished: _____

Source
Bought ○   Loaned ○
From: _____

Author: _____

Publisher: _____   Pub. date _____

Page count: _____

○ Fiction   ○ Non-fiction

Genre: _____   Subject: _____

My Review: _____

_____

_____

_____

_____

_____

_____

_____

_____

_____

_____

_____

_____

Inspiration Tree

Why I read it?
_____
⬇
It inspired me to
(read/learn/visit)?
_____
⬇
Who will I
recommend it to?
_____

✳ Ratings ✳

Plot: 1 2 3 4 5
Characters:
1 2 3 4 5
Ease of reading:
1 2 3 4 5

Overall
☹ 😐 ☺

Great quotes from this book.

Paperback ○   Hardback ○   e-book ○   Audiobook ○

Title:

5

Author: _____

Publisher: _____   Pub. date _____

Page count: _____

○ Fiction   ○ Non-fiction

Genre: _____   Subject: _____

Dates
Started: _____
Finished: _____

Source
Bought ○   Loaned ○
From: _____

My Review: _____

_____

_____

_____

_____

_____

_____

_____

_____

_____

_____

_____

Inspiration Tree

Why I read it?
_____
↓
It inspired me to
(read/learn/visit)?
_____
_____
↓
Who will I
recommend it to?
_____

Great quotes from this book:

✳ Ratings ✳

Plot: 1 2 3 4 5
Characters:
1 2 3 4 5
Ease of reading:
1 2 3 4 5

Overall

6

Paperback ○   Hardback ○   e-book ○   Audiobook ○

Title:

Dates
Started: _____
Finished: _____

Source
Bought ○ Loaned ○
From: _____

💡

Inspiration Tree

Why I read it?
_____
⬇
It inspired me to
(read/learn/visit)?
_____
⬇
Who will I
recommend it to?
_____

✳ Ratings ✳

Plot: 1 2 3 4 5
Characters:
1 2 3 4 5
Ease of reading:
1 2 3 4 5
Overall
☹ 😐 ☺

Author: _____
Publisher: _____   **Pub. date** _____
Page count: _____
○ Fiction   ○ Non-fiction
  Genre: _____   Subject: _____

My Review: _____

_____
_____
_____
_____
_____
_____
_____
_____
_____
_____
_____
_____
_____

Great quotes from this book:

Paperback ○   Hardback ○   e-book ○   Audiobook ○

Title:

7

Author: _____

Publisher: _____   Pub. date _____

Page count: _____

○ Fiction   ○ Non-fiction

Genre: _____   Subject: _____

My Review: _____

_____

_____

_____

_____

_____

_____

_____

_____

_____

_____

_____

_____

_____

Great quotes from this book:

Dates
Started: _____
Finished: _____

Source
Bought ○   Loaned ○
From: _____

Inspiration Tree

Why I read it?
_____
↓
It inspired me to
(read/learn/visit)?
_____
_____
↓
Who will I
recommend it to?
_____

✱ Ratings ✱

Plot: 1 2 3 4 5
Characters:
1 2 3 4 5
Ease of reading:
1 2 3 4 5
Overall
☹ 😐 🙂

8

Paperback ○   Hardback ○   e-book ○   Audiobook ○

Title:

Dates
Started: _____
Finished: _____

Source
Bought ○ Loaned ○
From: _____

Author: _____
Publisher: _____ Pub. date _____
Page count: _____
○ Fiction   ○ Non-fiction
  Genre: _____   Subject: _____

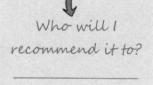

Inspiration Tree

Why I read it?
_____
↓
It inspired me to
(read/learn/visit)?
_____
↓
Who will I
recommend it to?
_____

✳ Ratings ✳

Plot: 1 2 3 4 5
Characters:
1 2 3 4 5
Ease of reading:
1 2 3 4 5
Overall
☹ 😐 ☺

My Review: ....
_____
_____
_____
_____
_____
_____
_____
_____
_____
_____
_____
_____
_____
_____

Great quotes from this book:

Paperback ○   Hardback ○   e-book ○   Audiobook ○

Title:

9

Author: _____

Publisher: _____   Pub. date _____

Page count: _____

○ Fiction   ○ Non-fiction

  Genre: _____   Subject: _____

Dates
Started: _____
Finished: _____

Source
Bought ○   Loaned ○
From: _____

My Review: _____

_____
_____
_____
_____
_____
_____
_____
_____
_____
_____
_____
_____
_____

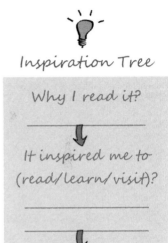

Inspiration Tree

Why I read it?
_____
⬇
It inspired me to
(read/learn/visit)?
_____
_____
⬇
Who will I
recommend it to?
_____

✳ Ratings ✳

Plot. 1 2 3 4 5
Characters.
1 2 3 4 5
Ease of reading:
1 2 3 4 5
Overall
☹ 😐 🙂

Great quotes from this book:

10

Title:

Dates
Started: _____
Finished: _____

Source
Bought ○ Loaned ○
From: _____

💡

Inspiration Tree

Why I read it?
_____
⬇
It inspired me to
(read/learn/visit)?
_____
⬇
Who will I
recommend it to?
_____

✳ Ratings ✳

Plot: 1 2 3 4 5
Characters:
1 2 3 4 5
Ease of reading:
1 2 3 4 5
Overall
☹ 😐 🙂

Author: _____
Publisher: _____   Pub. date _____
Page count: _____
○ Fiction   ○ Non-fiction
  Genre: _____   Subject: _____

My Review: _____
_____
_____
_____
_____
_____
_____
_____
_____
_____
_____
_____
_____
_____
_____

Great quotes from this book:

Paperback ○   Hardback ○   e-book ○   Audiobook ○

11

Title:

Author: _____

Publisher: _____ Pub. date _____

Page count: _____

○ Fiction   ○ Non-fiction
  Genre: _____   Subject: _____

Dates
Started: _____
Finished: _____

Source
Bought ○ Loaned ○
From: _____

My Review: _____

_____
_____
_____
_____
_____
_____
_____
_____
_____
_____
_____
_____

Inspiration Tree

Why I read it?
_____

It inspired me to
(read/learn/visit)?
_____

Who will I
recommend it to?
_____

Great quotes from this book:

✳ Ratings ✳

Plot: 1 2 3 4 5
Characters:
1 2 3 4 5
Ease of reading:
1 2 3 4 5
Overall
☹ 😐 ☺

12

Paperback ○   Hardback ○   e-book ○   Audiobook ○

Title:

Dates
Started: _____
Finished: _____

Source
Bought ○   Loaned ○
From: _____

Author: _____
Publisher: _____   Pub. date _____
Page count: _____
○ Fiction   ○ Non-fiction
   Genre: _____   Subject: _____

My Review: _____
_____
_____
_____
_____
_____
_____
_____
_____
_____
_____
_____
_____
_____

Inspiration Tree

Why I read it?
_____
⬇
It inspired me to
(read/learn/visit)?
_____
_____
⬇
Who will I
recommend it to?
_____

✳ Ratings ✳

Plot: 1 2 3 4 5
Characters:
1 2 3 4 5
Ease of reading:
1 2 3 4 5
Overall
☹ 😐 ☺

Great quotes from this book:

Paperback ○   Hardback ○   e-book ○   Audiobook ○

Title:

Author: _____

Publisher: _____   Pub. date _____

Page count: _____

○ Fiction   ○ Non-fiction

   Genre: _____   Subject: _____

Dates
Started: _____
Finished: _____

Source
Bought ○   Loaned ○
From: _____

My Review: _____

_____
_____
_____
_____
_____
_____
_____
_____
_____
_____
_____
_____

Great quotes from this book:

Inspiration Tree

Why I read it?
_____
⬇
It inspired me to
(read/learn/visit)?
_____
_____
⬇
Who will I
recommend it to?
_____

✳ Ratings ✳

Plot: 1 2 3 4 5
Characters:
1 2 3 4 5
Ease of reading:
1 2 3 4 5
Overall
☹ 😐 🙂

14

Title:

Dates
Started: _____
Finished: _____

Source
Bought ○ Loaned ○
From: _____

Author: _____
Publisher: _____   Pub. date _____
Page count: _____
○ Fiction   ○ Non-fiction
  Genre: _____   Subject: _____

Inspiration Tree

Why I read it?
_____
⬇
It inspired me to
(read/learn/visit)?
_____
⬇
Who will I
recommend it to?
_____

My Review:

_____
_____
_____
_____
_____
_____
_____
_____
_____
_____
_____
_____
_____
_____

✳ Ratings ✳

Plot: 1 2 3 4 5
Characters:
1 2 3 4 5
Ease of reading:
1 2 3 4 5
Overall
☹ 😐 ☺

Great quotes from this book:

Paperback ○ Hardback ○ e-book ○ Audiobook ○

15

Title:

Author: ____________________

Publisher: ____________________ Pub. date ____________

Page count: ____________

○ Fiction

Genre: ____________

○ Non-fiction

Subject: ____________

Dates

Started: ____________

Finished: ____________

Source

Bought ○ Loaned ○

From: ____________

My Review: ____________________

Inspiration Tree

Why I read it?

____

It inspired me to (read/learn/visit)?

____

____

Who will I recommend it to?

____

✱ Ratings ✱

Plot: 1 2 3 4 5

Characters:

1 2 3 4 5

Ease of reading:

1 2 3 4 5

Overall

Great quotes from this book:

16

Title:

Dates
Started: _____
Finished: _____

Source
Bought ○　Loaned ○
From: _____

Author: _____

Publisher: _____　Pub. date _____

Page count: _____

○ Fiction　　　　　　　　　○ Non-fiction
　Genre: _____　　Subject: _____

💡

Inspiration Tree

Why I read it?
_____
⬇
It inspired me to
(read/learn/visit)?
_____
⬇
Who will I
recommend it to?
_____

My Review: _____

_____
_____
_____
_____
_____
_____
_____
_____
_____
_____
_____
_____
_____

✳ Ratings ✳

Plot: 1　2　3　4　5
Characters:
1　2　3　4　5
Ease of reading:
1　2　3　4　5
Overall
☹　😐　☺

Great quotes from this book:

Paperback ○   Hardback ○   e-book ○   Audiobook ○

17

Title:

Author: _____

Publisher: _____ Pub. date _____

Page count: _____

○ Fiction   ○ Non-fiction

Genre: _____ Subject: _____

Dates
Started: _____
Finished: _____

Source
Bought ○   Loaned ○
From: _____

My Review: _____

_____
_____
_____
_____
_____
_____
_____
_____
_____
_____
_____
_____
_____

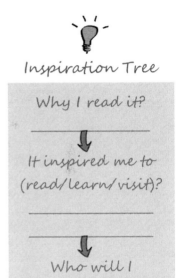

Inspiration Tree

Why I read it?
_____
↓
It inspired me to
(read/learn/visit)?
_____
_____
↓
Who will I
recommend it to?
_____

Great quotes from this book:

✳ Ratings ✳

Plot: 1 2 3 4 5
Characters:
1 2 3 4 5
Ease of reading:
1 2 3 4 5
Overall
☹ 😐 ☺

Paperback ○   Hardback ○   e-book ○   Audiobook ○

Title:

Dates
Started: _____
Finished: _____

Source
Bought ○   Loaned ○
From: _____

Author: _____
Publisher: _____   Pub. date _____
Page count: _____
○ Fiction   ○ Non-fiction
  Genre: _____   Subject: _____

My Review: _____
_____
_____
_____
_____
_____
_____
_____
_____
_____
_____
_____
_____
_____
_____

Inspiration Tree

Why I read it?
_____
↓
It inspired me to
(read/learn/visit)?
_____
↓
Who will I
recommend it to?
_____

✳ Ratings ✳

Plot: 1 2 3 4 5
Characters:
1 2 3 4 5
Ease of reading:
1 2 3 4 5
Overall
☹ 😐 🙂

Great quotes from this book:

Paperback ○   Hardback ○   e-book ○   Audiobook ○

Title:

19

Author: _____

Publisher: _____ Pub. date _____

Page count: _____

○ Fiction   ○ Non-fiction

  Genre: _____   Subject: _____

Dates
Started: _____
Finished: _____

Source
Bought ○   Loaned ○
From: _____

My Review: _____

_____

_____

_____

_____

_____

_____

_____

_____

_____

_____

_____

_____

Inspiration Tree

Why I read it?
_____
↓
It inspired me to
(read/learn/visit)?
_____
_____
↓
Who will I
recommend it to?
_____

Great quotes from this book:

✷ Ratings ✷

Plot: 1 2 3 4 5
Characters:
1 2 3 4 5
Ease of reading:
1 2 3 4 5
Overall
☹ 😐 🙂

20

Paperback ○   Hardback ○   e-book ○   Audiobook ○

Title:

Dates
Started: _____
Finished: _____

Source
Bought ○ Loaned ○
From: _____

Author: _____
Publisher: _____   Pub. date _____
Page count: _____
○ Fiction   ○ Non-fiction
   Genre: _____   Subject: _____

💡

Inspiration Tree

Why I read it?
_____
↓
It inspired me to
(read/learn/visit)?
_____
↓
Who will I
recommend it to?
_____

My Review: _____
_____
_____
_____
_____
_____
_____
_____
_____
_____
_____
_____
_____
_____

✳ Ratings ✳

Plot: 1 2 3 4 5
Characters:
1 2 3 4 5
Ease of reading:
1 2 3 4 5
Overall
☹ 😐 ☺

Great quotes from this book:

Paperback ○   Hardback ○   e-book ○   Audiobook ○

Title:

21

Author: _____

Publisher: _____ Pub. date _____

Page count: _____

○ Fiction   ○ Non-fiction

  Genre: _____   Subject: _____

Dates
Started: _____
Finished: _____

Source
Bought ○ Loaned ○
From: _____

My Review: _____

_____

_____

_____

_____

_____

_____

_____

_____

_____

_____

_____

_____

Inspiration Tree

Why I read it?
_____

It inspired me to
(read/learn/visit)?
_____
_____

Who will I
recommend it to?
_____

✳ Ratings ✳

Plot: 1 2 3 4 5
Characters:
1 2 3 4 5
Ease of reading:
1 2 3 4 5

Great quotes from this book:

Overall
☹ 😐 ☺

22

Title:

Author: _____

Publisher: _____   Pub. date _____

Page count: _____

○ Fiction   ○ Non-fiction

  Genre: _____   Subject: _____

Dates

Started: _____

Finished: _____

Source

Bought ○   Loaned ○

From: _____

Inspiration Tree

Why I read it?

_____

↓

It inspired me to
(read/learn/visit)?

_____

↓

Who will I
recommend it to?

_____

✳ Ratings ✳

Plot: 1 2 3 4 5

Characters:

1 2 3 4 5

Ease of reading:

1 2 3 4 5

Overall

☹ 😐 ☺

My Review: _____

_____

_____

_____

_____

_____

_____

_____

_____

_____

_____

_____

_____

Great quotes from this book:

Paperback ○   Hardback ○   e-book ○   Audiobook ○

Title:

23

Author: _____

Publisher: _____ Pub. date _____

Page count: _____

○ Fiction   ○ Non-fiction

  Genre: _____   Subject: _____

My Review: _____
_____
_____
_____
_____
_____
_____
_____
_____
_____
_____
_____
_____

Great quotes from this book:

Dates
Started: _____
Finished: _____

Source
Bought ○ Loaned ○
From: _____

Inspiration Tree

Why I read it?
_____
↓
It inspired me to
(read/learn/visit)?
_____
_____
↓
Who will I
recommend it to?
_____

✷ Ratings ✷

Plot: 1 2 3 4 5
Characters:
1 2 3 4 5
Ease of reading:
1 2 3 4 5
Overall
☹ 😐 ☺

24

Title:

Dates
Started: _____
Finished: _____

Source
Bought ○   Loaned ○
From: _____

Author: _____

Publisher: _____   Pub. date _____

Page count: _____

○ Fiction   ○ Non-fiction
  Genre: _____   Subject: _____

Inspiration Tree

Why I read it?
_____
⬇
It inspired me to
(read/learn/visit)?
_____
⬇
Who will I
recommend it to?
_____

✳ Ratings ✳

Plot: 1 2 3 4 5
Characters:
1 2 3 4 5
Ease of reading:
1 2 3 4 5
Overall
☹ 😐 ☺

My Review: _____
_____
_____
_____
_____
_____
_____
_____
_____
_____
_____
_____

Great quotes from this book:

Paperback ○   Hardback ○   e-book ○   Audiobook ○

Title:

Author: _____

Publisher: _____   Pub. date _____

Page count: _____

○ Fiction   ○ Non-fiction
  Genre: _____   Subject: _____

My Review: _____
_____
_____
_____
_____
_____
_____
_____
_____
_____
_____
_____

Great quotes from this book:

Dates
Started: _____
Finished: _____

Source
Bought ○   Loaned ○
From: _____

Inspiration Tree

Why I read it?
_____
↓
It inspired me to
(read/learn/visit)?
_____
_____
↓
Who will I
recommend it to?
_____

✳ Ratings ✳

Plot. 1 2 3 4 5
Characters:
1 2 3 4 5
Ease of reading:
1 2 3 4 5
Overall
☹ 😐 ☺

26

Title:

Dates
Started: _____
Finished: _____

Source
Bought ○   Loaned ○
From: _____

Inspiration Tree

Why I read it?
_____
⬇
It inspired me to
(read/learn/visit)?
_____
⬇
Who will I
recommend it to?
_____

✳ Ratings ✳

Plot: 1 2 3 4 5
Characters:
1 2 3 4 5
Ease of reading:
1 2 3 4 5
Overall
☹ 😐 ☺

Author: _____
Publisher: _____   Pub. date _____
Page count: _____
○ Fiction   ○ Non-fiction
   Genre: _____   Subject: _____

My Review: _____
_____
_____
_____
_____
_____
_____
_____
_____
_____
_____
_____
_____

Great quotes from this book:

Paperback ○   Hardback ○   e-book ○   Audiobook ○

Title:

27

Author: _____

Publisher: _____ Pub. date _____

Page count: _____

○ Fiction   ○ Non-fiction

  Genre: _____   Subject: _____

Dates
Started: _____
Finished: _____

Source
Bought ○ Loaned ○
From: _____

My Review: _____

_____
_____
_____
_____
_____
_____
_____
_____
_____
_____
_____
_____
_____
_____

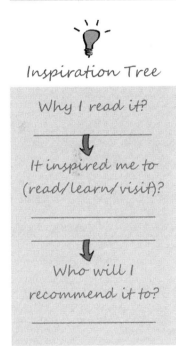

Inspiration Tree

Why I read it?
_____
↓
It inspired me to
(read/learn/visit)?
_____
_____
↓
Who will I
recommend it to?
_____

✳ Ratings ✳

Plot: 1 2 3 4 5
Characters:
1 2 3 4 5
Ease of reading:
1 2 3 4 5
Overall
☹ 😐 ☺

Great quotes from this book:

28

Paperback ○   Hardback ○   e-book ○   Audiobook ○

Title:

Dates
Started: _____
Finished: _____

Source
Bought ○   Loaned ○
From: _____

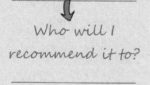

Inspiration Tree

Why I read it?
_____
⬇
It inspired me to
(read/learn/visit)?
_____
_____
⬇
Who will I
recommend it to?
_____

✳ Ratings ✳

Plot: 1 2 3 4 5
Characters:
1 2 3 4 5
Ease of reading:
1 2 3 4 5
Overall
☹ 😐 ☺

Author: _____
Publisher: _____   Pub. date _____
Page count: _____
○ Fiction   ○ Non-fiction
  Genre: _____   Subject: _____

My Review: _____

_____
_____
_____
_____
_____
_____
_____
_____
_____
_____
_____
_____

Great quotes from this book:

Paperback ○   Hardback ○   e-book ○   Audiobook ○

29

Title:

Author: _____

Publisher: _____ Pub. date _____

Page count: _____

○ Fiction   ○ Non-fiction

   Genre: _____   Subject: _____

Dates
Started: _____
Finished: _____

Source
Bought ○   Loaned ○
From: _____

My Review: _____
_____
_____
_____
_____
_____
_____
_____
_____
_____
_____
_____
_____
_____

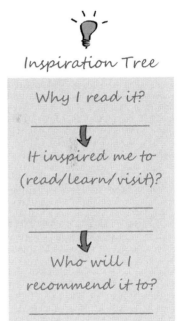

Inspiration Tree

Why I read it?
_____

It inspired me to
(read/learn/visit)?
_____
_____

Who will I
recommend it to?
_____

⁕ Ratings ⁕

Plot: 1 2 3 4 5
Characters:
1 2 3 4 5
Ease of reading:
1 2 3 4 5

Overall
☹ 😐 🙂

Great quotes from this book:

30

Title:

Author: _____

Publisher: _____   Pub. date _____

Page count: _____

○ Fiction   ○ Non-fiction

   Genre: _____   Subject: _____

My Review: ....

_____

_____

_____

_____

_____

_____

_____

_____

_____

_____

_____

_____

Dates

Started: _____

Finished: _____

Source

Bought ○   Loaned ○

From: _____

Inspiration Tree

Why I read it?

_____

⬇

It inspired me to
(read/learn/visit)?

_____

⬇

Who will I
recommend it to?

_____

✳ Ratings ✳

Plot: 1 2 3 4 5

Characters:
1 2 3 4 5

Ease of reading:
1 2 3 4 5

Overall

☹ 😐 ☺

Great quotes from this book:

Paperback ○   Hardback ○   e-book ○   Audiobook ○

Title:

31

Author: _____

Publisher: _____   Pub. date _____

Page count: _____

○ Fiction   ○ Non-fiction

  Genre: _____   Subject: _____

Dates
Started: _____
Finished: _____

Source
Bought ○ Loaned ○
From: _____

My Review: _____

_____

_____

_____

_____

_____

_____

_____

_____

_____

_____

_____

Inspiration Tree

Why I read it?
_____
↓
It inspired me to
(read/learn/visit)?
_____
_____
↓
Who will I
recommend it to?
_____

✳ Ratings ✳

Plot: 1 2 3 4 5
Characters:
1 2 3 4 5
Ease of reading:
1 2 3 4 5
Overall
☹ 😐 🙂

Great quotes from this book:

32

Title:

Dates
Started: _____
Finished: _____

Source
Bought ○ Loaned ○
From: _____

Inspiration Tree

Why I read it?
_____

↓

It inspired me to
(read/learn/visit)?
_____

↓

Who will I
recommend it to?
_____

✳ Ratings ✳

Plot: 1 2 3 4 5
Characters:
1 2 3 4 5
Ease of reading:
1 2 3 4 5
Overall
☹ 😐 ☺

Author: _____
Publisher: _____   Pub. date _____
Page count: _____
○ Fiction   ○ Non-fiction
  Genre: _____   Subject: _____

My Review: _____
_____
_____
_____
_____
_____
_____
_____
_____
_____
_____
_____
_____

Great quotes from this book:

Paperback ○   Hardback ○   e-book ○   Audiobook ○

33

Title:

Author: _____

Publisher: _____ Pub. date _____

Page count: _____

○ Fiction   ○ Non-fiction

Genre: _____ Subject: _____

Dates
Started: _____
Finished: _____

Source
Bought ○ Loaned ○
From: _____

My Review: _____

_____

_____

_____

_____

_____

_____

_____

_____

_____

_____

_____

Inspiration Tree

Why I read it?
_____
↓
It inspired me to
(read/learn/visit)?
_____
_____
↓
Who will I
recommend it to?
_____

Great quotes from this book:

✳ Ratings ✳

Plot: 1 2 3 4 5
Characters:
1 2 3 4 5
Ease of reading:
1 2 3 4 5
Overall
☹ 😐 🙂

34

Title:

Dates
Started: _____
Finished: _____

Source
Bought ○   Loaned ○
From: _____

💡

Inspiration Tree

Why I read it?
_____
⬇
It inspired me to
(read/learn/visit)?
_____
_____
⬇
Who will I
recommend it to?
_____

✳ Ratings ✳

Plot: 1 2 3 4 5
Characters:
1 2 3 4 5
Ease of reading:
1 2 3 4 5
Overall
😞 😐 😊

Author: _____
Publisher: _____   Pub. date _____
Page count: _____
○ Fiction   ○ Non-fiction
  Genre: _____   Subject: _____

My Review:

_____
_____
_____
_____
_____
_____
_____
_____
_____
_____
_____
_____
_____

Great quotes from this book:

Paperback ○   Hardback ○   e-book ○   Audiobook ○

35

Title:

Author: _____

Publisher: _____   Pub. date _____

Page count: _____

○ Fiction   ○ Non-fiction

  Genre: _____   Subject: _____

Dates
Started: _____
Finished: _____

Source
Bought ○   Loaned ○
From: _____

My Review: _____

....

....

....

....

....

....

....

....

....

....

....

....

Inspiration Tree

Why I read it?
_____

It inspired me to
(read/learn/visit)?

_____

Who will I
recommend it to?

_____

✳ Ratings ✳

Plot. 1 2 3 4 5
Characters.
1 2 3 4 5
Ease of reading:
1 2 3 4 5
Overall
☹ 😐 ☺

Great quotes from this book:

36

Title:

Dates
Started: _____
Finished: _____

Source
Bought ○ Loaned ○
From: _____

Author: _____
Publisher: _____ Pub. date _____
Page count: _____
○ Fiction   ○ Non-fiction
  Genre: _____   Subject: _____

My Review: _____
_____
_____
_____
_____
_____
_____
_____
_____
_____
_____
_____
_____
_____
_____

Inspiration Tree

Why I read it?
_____
⬇
It inspired me to
(read/learn/visit)?
_____
_____
⬇
Who will I
recommend it to?
_____

✳ Ratings ✳

Plot: 1 2 3 4 5
Characters:
1 2 3 4 5
Ease of reading:
1 2 3 4 5
Overall
☹ 😐 🙂

Great quotes from this book:

Paperback ○   Hardback ○   e-book ○   Audiobook ○

Title:

Author: _____

Publisher: _____ Pub. date _____

Page count: _____

○ Fiction   ○ Non-fiction
  Genre: _____   Subject: _____

Dates
Started: _____
Finished: _____

Source
Bought ○   Loaned ○
From: _____

My Review: _____
_____
_____
_____
_____
_____
_____
_____
_____
_____
_____
_____
_____
_____

Inspiration Tree

Why I read it?
_____
⬇
It inspired me to
(read/learn/visit)?
_____
_____
⬇
Who will I
recommend it to?
_____

✳ Ratings ✳

Plot. 1 2 3 4 5
Characters:
1 2 3 4 5
Ease of reading:
1 2 3 4 5
Overall
☹ 😐 🙂

Great quotes from this book:

38

Title:

Author: _____

Publisher: _____   Pub. date _____

Page count: _____

○ Fiction   ○ Non-fiction

Genre: _____   Subject: _____

Dates

Started: _____

Finished: _____

Source

Bought ○   Loaned ○

From: _____

Inspiration Tree

Why I read it?

_____

⬇

It inspired me to
(read/learn/visit)?

_____

⬇

Who will I
recommend it to?

_____

✳ Ratings ✳

Plot: 1 2 3 4 5

Characters:

1 2 3 4 5

Ease of reading:

1 2 3 4 5

Overall

☹ 😐 ☺

My Review: _____

_____

_____

_____

_____

_____

_____

_____

_____

_____

_____

_____

Great quotes from this book:

Paperback ○   Hardback ○   e-book ○   Audiobook ○

39

Title:

Author: _____

Publisher: _____ Pub. date _____

Page count: _____

○ Fiction   ○ Non-fiction

   Genre: _____   Subject: _____

Dates
Started: _____
Finished: _____

Source
Bought ○ Loaned ○
From: _____

My Review: _____

_____

_____

_____

_____

_____

_____

_____

_____

_____

_____

_____

_____

Inspiration Tree

Why I read it?
_____
↓
It inspired me to
(read/learn/visit)?
_____
↓
Who will I
recommend it to?
_____

✳ Ratings ✳

Plot: 1 2 3 4 5
Characters:
1 2 3 4 5
Ease of reading:
1 2 3 4 5
Overall
☹ 😐 🙂

Great quotes from this book:

40

Title:

Dates

Started: _____

Finished: _____

Source

Bought ○ Loaned ○

From: _____

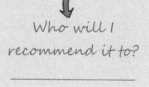

Inspiration Tree

Why I read it?

_____

⬇

It inspired me to
(read/learn/visit)?

_____

⬇

Who will I
recommend it to?

_____

✳ Ratings ✳

Plot: 1 2 3 4 5

Characters:
1 2 3 4 5

Ease of reading:
1 2 3 4 5

Overall
☹ 😐 ☺

Author: _____

Publisher: _____   Pub. date _____

Page count: _____

○ Fiction   ○ Non-fiction

  Genre: _____   Subject: _____

My Review: _____

_____

_____

_____

_____

_____

_____

_____

_____

_____

_____

_____

_____

Great quotes from this book:

Paperback ○   Hardback ○   e-book ○   Audiobook ○

41

Title:

Author: _____

Publisher: _____ Pub. date _____

Page count: _____

○ Fiction   ○ Non-fiction

  Genre: _____   Subject: _____

Dates
Started: _____
Finished: _____

Source
Bought ○ Loaned ○
From: _____

My Review: _____
_____
_____
_____
_____
_____
_____
_____
_____
_____
_____
_____
_____

Inspiration Tree

Why I read it?
_____
↓
It inspired me to
(read/learn/visit)?
_____
_____
↓
Who will I
recommend it to?
_____

✖ Ratings ✖

Plot: 1 2 3 4 5
Characters:
1 2 3 4 5
Ease of reading:
1 2 3 4 5

Overall
☹ 😐 🙂

Great quotes from this book:

42

Title:

Dates
Started: _____
Finished: _____

Source
Bought ○   Loaned ○
From: _____

Inspiration Tree

Why I read it?
_____
⬇
It inspired me to
(read/learn/visit)?
_____
⬇
Who will I
recommend it to?
_____

✹ Ratings ✹

Plot: 1 2 3 4 5
Characters:
1 2 3 4 5
Ease of reading:
1 2 3 4 5
Overall
☹ 😐 ☺

Author: _____
Publisher: _____   Pub. date _____
Page count: _____
○ Fiction   ○ Non-fiction
   Genre: _____   Subject: _____

My Review: _____

_____
_____
_____
_____
_____
_____
_____
_____
_____
_____
_____
_____
_____

Great quotes from this book:

Paperback ○ Hardback ○ e-book ○ Audiobook ○

43

Title:

Author:

Publisher: Pub. date

Page count:

○ Fiction ○ Non-fiction

Genre: Subject:

My Review:

Great quotes from this book:

Dates

Started:

Finished:

Source

Bought ○ Loaned ○

From:

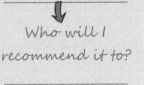

Inspiration Tree

Why I read it?

It inspired me to (read/learn/visit)?

Who will I recommend it to?

⁎ Ratings ⁎

Plot: 1 2 3 4 5

Characters: 1 2 3 4 5

Ease of reading: 1 2 3 4 5

Overall

44

Title:

Author: _____

Publisher: _____　　Pub. date _____

Page count: _____

○ Fiction　　　　　　　　　○ Non-fiction

　Genre: _____　　　Subject: _____

Dates
Started: _____
Finished: _____

Source
Bought ○　Loaned ○
From: _____

Inspiration Tree

Why I read it?
_____
↓
It inspired me to
(read/learn/visit)?
_____
↓
Who will I
recommend it to?
_____

✳ Ratings ✳
Plot: 1 2 3 4 5
Characters:
1 2 3 4 5
Ease of reading:
1 2 3 4 5
Overall
☹ 😐 ☺

My Review:

_____
_____
_____
_____
_____
_____
_____
_____
_____
_____
_____
_____

Great quotes from this book.

Paperback ○   Hardback ○   e-book ○   Audiobook ○

Title:

45

Author: _____

Publisher: _____ Pub. date _____

Page count: _____

○ Fiction   ○ Non-fiction
  Genre: _____   Subject: _____

Dates
Started: _____
Finished: _____

Source
Bought ○ Loaned ○
From: _____

My Review: _____

_____

_____

_____

_____

_____

_____

_____

_____

_____

_____

_____

_____

Inspiration Tree

Why I read it?
_____
⬇
It inspired me to
(read/learn/visit)?
_____
⬇
Who will I
recommend it to?
_____

✳ Ratings ✳

Plot: 1 2 3 4 5
Characters:
1 2 3 4 5
Ease of reading:
1 2 3 4 5
Overall
☹ 😐 ☺

Great quotes from this book:

46

Title:

Author: _____

Publisher: _____   Pub. date _____

Page count: _____

○ Fiction   ○ Non-fiction

  Genre: _____   Subject: _____

Dates
Started: _____

Finished: _____

Source
Bought ○   Loaned ○

From: _____

Inspiration Tree

Why I read it?
_____
↓
It inspired me to (read/learn/visit)?
_____
_____
↓
Who will I recommend it to?
_____

✳ Ratings ✳

Plot: 1 2 3 4 5

Characters:
1 2 3 4 5

Ease of reading:
1 2 3 4 5

Overall
☹ 😐 ☺

My Review:
_____
_____
_____
_____
_____
_____
_____
_____
_____
_____
_____
_____
_____

Great quotes from this book:

Paperback ○   Hardback ○   e-book ○   Audiobook ○

Title:

47

Author: _____

Publisher: _____ Pub. date _____

Page count: _____

○ Fiction   ○ Non-fiction

Genre: _____   Subject: _____

Dates
Started: _____
Finished: _____

Source
Bought ○   Loaned ○
From: _____

My Review: _____

_____

_____

_____

_____

_____

_____

_____

_____

_____

_____

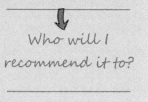

Inspiration Tree

Why I read it?
_____
↓
It inspired me to
(read/learn/visit)?
_____
_____
↓
Who will I
recommend it to?
_____

✳ Ratings ✳

Plot: 1 2 3 4 5
Characters:
1 2 3 4 5
Ease of reading:
1 2 3 4 5

Overall

Great quotes from this book:

48

Title:

Dates
Started: _____
Finished: _____

Source
Bought ○ Loaned ○
From: _____

Author: _____

Publisher: _____   Pub. date _____

Page count: _____

○ Fiction   ○ Non-fiction
  Genre: _____   Subject: _____

Inspiration Tree

Why I read it?
_____

It inspired me to (read/learn/visit)?
_____

Who will I recommend it to?
_____

My Review: _____

_____

_____

_____

_____

_____

_____

_____

_____

_____

_____

_____

_____

_____

_____

✳ Ratings ✳

Plot: 1 2 3 4 5

Characters:
1 2 3 4 5

Ease of reading:
1 2 3 4 5

Overall
☹ 😐 ☺

Great quotes from this book:

Paperback ○   Hardback ○   e-book ○   Audiobook ○

Title:

49

Author: _____

Publisher: _____ Pub. date _____

Page count: _____

○ Fiction   ○ Non-fiction

   Genre: _____   Subject: _____

My Review: _____

_____

_____

_____

_____

_____

_____

_____

_____

_____

_____

_____

_____

_____

_____

Great quotes from this book:

Dates

Started: _____

Finished: _____

Source

Bought ○   Loaned ○

From: _____

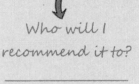

Inspiration Tree

Why I read it?

_____

↓

It inspired me to
(read/learn/visit)?

_____

_____

↓

Who will I
recommend it to?

_____

✳ Ratings ✳

Plot: 1 2 3 4 5

Characters:
1 2 3 4 5

Ease of reading:
1 2 3 4 5

Overall

50

Title:

Author: _____

Publisher: _____   Pub. date _____

Page count: _____

○ Fiction   ○ Non-fiction

　Genre: _____   Subject: _____

Dates
Started: _____
Finished: _____

Source
Bought ○ Loaned ○
From: _____

Inspiration Tree

Why I read it?
_____
⬇
It inspired me to
(read/learn/visit)?
_____
⬇
Who will I
recommend it to?
_____

✳ Ratings ✳
Plot: 1 2 3 4 5
Characters:
1 2 3 4 5
Ease of reading:
1 2 3 4 5
Overall
☹ 😐 ☺

My Review:

_____
_____
_____
_____
_____
_____
_____
_____
_____
_____
_____
_____
_____

Great quotes from this book:

Paperback ○   Hardback ○   e-book ○   Audiobook ○

Title:

51

Author: _____

Publisher: _____ Pub. date _____

Page count: _____

○ Fiction   ○ Non-fiction

   Genre: _____   Subject: _____

Dates
Started: _____
Finished: _____
Source
Bought ○ Loaned ○
From: _____

My Review: _____

_____

_____

_____

_____

_____

_____

_____

_____

_____

_____

_____

Inspiration Tree

Why I read it?
_____

It inspired me to
(read/learn/visit)?
_____

Who will I
recommend it to?
_____

Great quotes from this book:

✳ Ratings ✳

Plot: 1 2 3 4 5
Characters:
1 2 3 4 5
Ease of reading:
1 2 3 4 5
Overall
☹ 😐 🙂

52

Title:

Dates
Started: _____
Finished: _____

Source
Bought ○ Loaned ○
From: _____

Author: _____
Publisher: _____ Pub. date _____
Page count: _____
○ Fiction   ○ Non-fiction
  Genre: _____   Subject: _____

💡

Inspiration Tree

Why I read it?
_____
⬇
It inspired me to
(read/learn/visit)?
_____
⬇
Who will I
recommend it to?
_____

My Review: _____
_____
_____
_____
_____
_____
_____
_____
_____
_____
_____
_____
_____

✳ Ratings ✳

Plot: 1 2 3 4 5
Characters:
1 2 3 4 5
Ease of reading:
1 2 3 4 5
Overall
☹ 😐 ☺

Great quotes from this book:

Paperback ○   Hardback ○   e-book ○   Audiobook ○

Title:

53

Author: _____

Publisher: _____ Pub. date _____

Page count: _____

○ Fiction   ○ Non-fiction

Genre: _____   Subject: _____

Dates
Started: _____
Finished: _____

Source
Bought ○ Loaned ○

From: _____

My Review: _____

_____

_____

_____

_____

_____

_____

_____

_____

_____

_____

_____

Inspiration Tree

Why I read it?
_____
↓
It inspired me to
(read/learn/visit)?
_____
↓
Who will I
recommend it to?
_____

✳ Ratings ✳

Plot: 1 2 3 4 5
Characters:
1 2 3 4 5
Ease of reading:
1 2 3 4 5
Overall
☹ 😐 ☺

Great quotes from this book:

Paperback ○   Hardback ○   e-book ○   Audiobook ○

Title:

Dates
Started: _____
Finished: _____

Source
Bought ○ Loaned ○
From: _____

Inspiration Tree

Why I read it?
_____
⬇
It inspired me to
(read/learn/visit)?
_____
⬇
Who will I
recommend it to?
_____

✳ Ratings ✳

Plot: 1 2 3 4 5
Characters:
1 2 3 4 5
Ease of reading:
1 2 3 4 5
Overall
☹ 😐 🙂

Author: _____
Publisher: _____   Pub. date _____
Page count: _____
○ Fiction   ○ Non-fiction
  Genre: _____   Subject: _____

My Review: _____
_____
_____
_____
_____
_____
_____
_____
_____
_____
_____
_____
_____

Great quotes from this book:

Paperback ○   Hardback ○   e-book ○   Audiobook ○

Title:

55

Author: _____

Publisher: _____   Pub. date _____

Page count: _____

○ Fiction   ○ Non-fiction

  Genre: _____   Subject: _____

My Review:

_____
_____
_____
_____
_____
_____
_____
_____
_____
_____
_____
_____
_____
_____

Great quotes from this book:

Dates
Started: _____
Finished: _____

Source
Bought ○   Loaned ○
From: _____

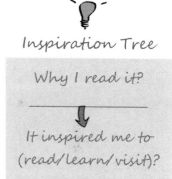

Inspiration Tree

Why I read it?
_____
↓
It inspired me to
(read/learn/visit)?
_____
_____
↓
Who will I
recommend it to?
_____

✳ Ratings ✳

Plot: 1 2 3 4 5
Characters:
1 2 3 4 5
Ease of reading:
1 2 3 4 5
Overall
☹ 😐 🙂

56

Title:

Dates
Started: _____
Finished: _____

Source
Bought ○ Loaned ○
From: _____

💡

Inspiration Tree

Why I read it?
_____
⬇
It inspired me to
(read/learn/visit)?
_____
⬇
Who will I
recommend it to?
_____

✳ Ratings ✳

Plot: 1 2 3 4 5
Characters:
1 2 3 4 5
Ease of reading:
1 2 3 4 5
Overall
☹ 😐 ☺

Author: _____
Publisher: _____   Pub. date _____
Page count: _____
○ Fiction   ○ Non-fiction
  Genre: _____   Subject: _____

My Review: _____
_____
_____
_____
_____
_____
_____
_____
_____
_____
_____
_____
_____
_____

Great quotes from this book:

Paperback ○   Hardback ○   e-book ○   Audiobook ○

Title:

57

Author: _____

Publisher: _____ Pub. date _____

Page count: _____

○ Fiction   ○ Non-fiction

  Genre: _____   Subject: _____

Dates
Started: _____
Finished: _____

Source
Bought ○ Loaned ○
From: _____

My Review: _____

_____

_____

_____

_____

_____

_____

_____

_____

_____

_____

_____

_____

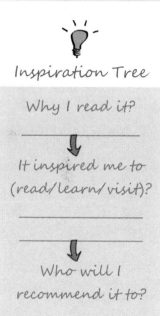

Inspiration Tree

Why I read it?
_____
↓
It inspired me to
(read/learn/visit)?
_____
_____
↓
Who will I
recommend it to?
_____

✹ Ratings ✹

Plot: 1 2 3 4 5
Characters:
1 2 3 4 5
Ease of reading:
1 2 3 4 5
Overall
☹ 😐 😊

Great quotes from this book:

58

Title:

Dates
Started: _____
Finished: _____

Source
Bought ○   Loaned ○
From: _____

Author: _____

Publisher: _____   Pub. date _____

Page count: _____

○ Fiction   ○ Non-fiction

  Genre: _____   Subject: _____

My Review: _____

_____

_____

_____

_____

_____

_____

_____

_____

_____

_____

_____

_____

_____

Inspiration Tree

Why I read it?
_____
↓
It inspired me to
(read/learn/visit)?
_____
↓
Who will I
recommend it to?
_____

✳ Ratings ✳

Plot: 1 2 3 4 5
Characters:
1 2 3 4 5
Ease of reading:
1 2 3 4 5
Overall
☹ 😐 🙂

Great quotes from this book:

Paperback ○   Hardback ○   e-book ○   Audiobook ○

59

Title:

Author: _____

Publisher: _____   Pub. date _____

Page count: _____

○ Fiction   ○ Non-fiction
  Genre: _____   Subject: _____

Dates
Started: _____
Finished: _____

Source
Bought ○   Loaned ○
From: _____

My Review: _____
_____
_____
_____
_____
_____
_____
_____
_____
_____
_____
_____
_____

Inspiration Tree

Why I read it?
_____
↓
It inspired me to
(read/learn/visit)?
_____
_____
↓
Who will I
recommend it to?
_____

Great quotes from this book:

✳ Ratings ✳

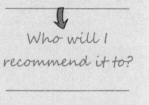

Plot: 1 2 3 4 5
Characters:
1 2 3 4 5
Ease of reading:
1 2 3 4 5
Overall
☹ 😐 ☺

60

Title:

Dates
Started: _____
Finished: _____

Source
Bought ○   Loaned ○
From: _____

Author: _____

Publisher: _____   Pub. date _____

Page count: _____

○ Fiction   ○ Non-fiction

  Genre: _____   Subject: _____

💡

Inspiration Tree

Why I read it?
_____
⬇
It inspired me to
(read/learn/visit)?
_____
_____
⬇
Who will I
recommend it to?
_____

My Review: _____

_____
_____
_____
_____
_____
_____
_____
_____
_____
_____
_____
_____
_____

✳ Ratings ✳

Plot: 1 2 3 4 5

Characters:
1 2 3 4 5

Ease of reading:
1 2 3 4 5

Overall
☹ 😐 ☺

Great quotes from this book:

Paperback ○　　Hardback ○　　e-book ○　　Audiobook ○

61

Title:

Author: _____

Publisher: _____ Pub. date _____

Page count: _____

○ Fiction   ○ Non-fiction
  Genre: _____   Subject: _____

Dates
Started: _____
Finished: _____

Source
Bought ○　Loaned ○
From: _____

My Review:
_____
_____
_____
_____
_____
_____
_____
_____
_____
_____
_____
_____
_____

Inspiration Tree

Why I read it?
_____
↓
It inspired me to
(read/learn/visit)?
_____
↓
Who will I
recommend it to?
_____

✳ Ratings ✳

Plot: 1 2 3 4 5
Characters:
1 2 3 4 5
Ease of reading:
1 2 3 4 5

Overall
☹ 😐 ☺

Great quotes from this book:

62

Paperback ○   Hardback ○   e-book ○   Audiobook ○

Title:

Dates
Started: _____
Finished: _____

Source
Bought ○ Loaned ○
From: _____

Author: _____
Publisher: _____   Pub. date _____
Page count: _____
○ Fiction   ○ Non-fiction
  Genre: _____   Subject: _____

My Review:

💡
Inspiration Tree

Why I read it?
_____
⬇
It inspired me to
(read/learn/visit)?
_____
⬇
Who will I
recommend it to?
_____

✳ Ratings ✳

Plot: 1 2 3 4 5
Characters:
1 2 3 4 5
Ease of reading:
1 2 3 4 5
Overall
☹ 😐 🙂

Great quotes from this book:

Paperback ○   Hardback ○   e-book ○   Audiobook ○

Title:

63

Author: _____

Publisher: _____ Pub. date _____

Page count: _____

○ Fiction   ○ Non-fiction
  Genre: _____   Subject: _____

Dates
Started: _____
Finished: _____

Source
Bought ○   Loaned ○
From: _____

My Review: _____
_____
_____
_____
_____
_____
_____
_____
_____
_____
_____
_____
_____

Inspiration Tree

Why I read it?
_____
↓
It inspired me to
(read/learn/visit)?
_____
↓
Who will I
recommend it to?
_____

✳ Ratings ✳

Plot: 1 2 3 4 5
Characters:
1 2 3 4 5
Ease of reading:
1 2 3 4 5
Overall
☹ 😐 🙂

Great quotes from this book:

64

Paperback ○   Hardback ○   e-book ○   Audiobook ○

Title:

Dates
Started: _____
Finished: _____

Source
Bought ○ Loaned ○
From: _____

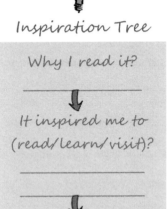

Inspiration Tree

Why I read it?
_____
↓
It inspired me to
(read/learn/visit)?
_____
↓
Who will I
recommend it to?
_____

✳ Ratings ✳

Plot: 1 2 3 4 5
Characters:
1 2 3 4 5
Ease of reading:
1 2 3 4 5
Overall
☹ 😐 🙂

Author: _____
Publisher: _____   Pub. date _____
Page count: _____
○ Fiction   ○ Non-fiction
  Genre: _____   Subject: _____

My Review: _____
_____
_____
_____
_____
_____
_____
_____
_____
_____
_____
_____

Great quotes from this book:

Paperback ○   Hardback ○   e-book ○   Audiobook ○

Title:

65

Author: _____

Publisher: _____ Pub. date _____

Page count: _____

○ Fiction   ○ Non-fiction

Genre: _____   Subject: _____

Dates
Started: _____
Finished: _____

Source
Bought ○ Loaned ○
From: _____

My Review: _____

_____

_____

_____

_____

_____

_____

_____

_____

_____

_____

_____

_____

_____

Great quotes from this book:

Inspiration Tree

Why I read it?
_____
↓
It inspired me to
(read/learn/visit)?
_____
_____
↓
Who will I
recommend it to?
_____

�֍ Ratings ✳

Plot: 1 2 3 4 5
Characters:
1 2 3 4 5
Ease of reading:
1 2 3 4 5
Overall
☹ 😐 ☺

66

Title:

Dates
Started: _____
Finished: _____

Source
Bought ○   Loaned ○
From: _____

Author: _____
Publisher: _____   Pub. date _____
Page count: _____
○ Fiction   ○ Non-fiction
  Genre: _____   Subject: _____

💡
Inspiration Tree

Why I read it?
_____
⬇
It inspired me to
(read/learn/visit)?
_____
⬇
Who will I
recommend it to?
_____

My Review: _____

_____
_____
_____
_____
_____
_____
_____
_____
_____
_____
_____
_____
_____

✴ Ratings ✴

Plot: 1 2 3 4 5
Characters:
1 2 3 4 5
Ease of reading:
1 2 3 4 5
Overall
☹ 😐 😊

Great quotes from this book:

Paperback ○   Hardback ○   e-book ○   Audiobook ○

67

Title:

Author: _____

Publisher: _____ Pub. date _____

Page count: _____

○ Fiction   ○ Non-fiction

  Genre: _____   Subject: _____

Dates
Started: _____
Finished: _____

Source
Bought ○ Loaned ○
From: _____

My Review: _____

_____
_____
_____
_____
_____
_____
_____
_____
_____
_____
_____
_____
_____

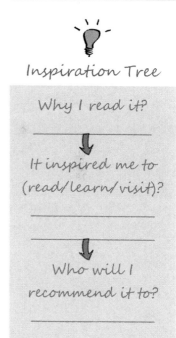

Inspiration Tree

Why I read it?
_____
↓
It inspired me to
(read/learn/visit)?
_____
_____
↓
Who will I
recommend it to?
_____

Great quotes from this book:

✳ Ratings ✳

Plot: 1 2 3 4 5
Characters:
1 2 3 4 5
Ease of reading:
1 2 3 4 5
Overall
☹ 😐 ☺

68

Title:

Author: _____

Publisher: _____　　Pub. date _____

Page count: _____

○ Fiction　　　　　　　　　　○ Non-fiction

　Genre: _____　　　　Subject: _____

Dates
Started: _____
Finished: _____

Source
Bought ○　Loaned ○
From: _____

Inspiration Tree

Why I read it?
_____

⬇

It inspired me to
(read/learn/visit)?
_____

_____

⬇

Who will I
recommend it to?
_____

✳ Ratings ✳

Plot: 1 2 3 4 5
Characters:
1 2 3 4 5
Ease of reading:
1 2 3 4 5
Overall
☹ 😐 🙂

My Review:
_____
_____
_____
_____
_____
_____
_____
_____
_____
_____
_____
_____
_____
_____
_____

Great quotes from this book:

Paperback ○   Hardback ○   e-book ○   Audiobook ○

69

Title:

Author: _____

Publisher: _____   Pub. date _____

Page count: _____

○ Fiction   ○ Non-fiction
   Genre: _____   Subject: _____

Dates
Started: _____
Finished: _____

Source
Bought ○ Loaned ○
From: _____

My Review: _____
_____
_____
_____
_____
_____
_____
_____
_____
_____
_____
_____
_____

Inspiration Tree

Why I read it?
_____
↓
It inspired me to
(read/learn/visit)?
_____
_____
↓
Who will I
recommend it to?
_____

✳ Ratings ✳

Plot: 1 2 3 4 5
Characters:
1 2 3 4 5
Ease of reading:
1 2 3 4 5
Overall
☹ 😐 ☺

Great quotes from this book:

70

Title:

Dates
Started: _____
Finished: _____

Source
Bought ○   Loaned ○
From: _____

Author: _____
Publisher: _____   Pub. date _____
Page count: _____
○ Fiction   ○ Non-fiction
   Genre: _____   Subject: _____

My Review:

_____
_____
_____
_____
_____
_____
_____
_____
_____
_____
_____
_____
_____

Inspiration Tree

Why I read it?
_____
⬇
It inspired me to
(read/learn/visit)?
_____
_____
⬇
Who will I
recommend it to?
_____

✳ Ratings ✳

Plot: 1 2 3 4 5
Characters:
1 2 3 4 5
Ease of reading:
1 2 3 4 5
Overall

Great quotes from this book:

Paperback ○   Hardback ○   e-book ○   Audiobook ○

Title:

71

Author: _____

Publisher: _____ Pub. date _____

Page count: _____

○ Fiction   ○ Non-fiction
   Genre: _____   Subject: _____

Dates
Started: _____
Finished: _____

Source
Bought ○   Loaned ○
From: _____

My Review: _____

_____
_____
_____
_____
_____
_____
_____
_____
_____
_____
_____
_____
_____

Great quotes from this book.

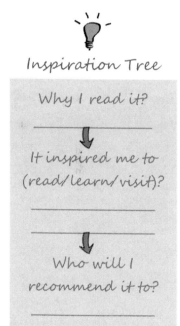

Inspiration Tree

Why I read it?
_____
⬇
It inspired me to
(read/learn/visit)?
_____
_____
⬇
Who will I
recommend it to?
_____

✳ Ratings ✳

Plot: 1 2 3 4 5
Characters:
1 2 3 4 5
Ease of reading:
1 2 3 4 5
Overall
☹ 😐 ☺

72

Title:

Dates
Started: _____
Finished: _____

Source
Bought ○   Loaned ○
From: _____

Author: _____
Publisher: _____ Pub. date _____
Page count: _____
○ Fiction   ○ Non-fiction
   Genre: _____   Subject: _____

💡

Inspiration Tree

Why I read it?
_____
⬇
It inspired me to (read/learn/visit)?
_____
⬇
Who will I recommend it to?
_____

My Review: _____
_____
_____
_____
_____
_____
_____
_____
_____
_____
_____
_____
_____
_____

✳ Ratings ✳

Plot: 1 2 3 4 5
Characters:
1 2 3 4 5
Ease of reading:
1 2 3 4 5
Overall
☹ 😐 ☺

Great quotes from this book:

Paperback ○   Hardback ○   e-book ○   Audiobook ○

Title:

73

Author: _____

Publisher: _____   Pub. date _____

Page count: _____

○ Fiction   ○ Non-fiction

Genre: _____   Subject: _____

Dates
Started: _____

Finished: _____

Source
Bought ○   Loaned ○

From: _____

My Review: _____

_____

_____

_____

_____

_____

_____

_____

_____

_____

_____

_____

_____

_____

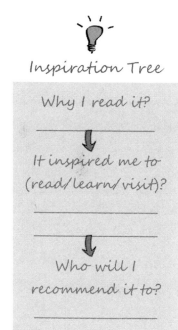

Inspiration Tree

Why I read it?

_____

↓

It inspired me to
(read/learn/visit)?

_____

_____

↓

Who will I
recommend it to?

_____

Great quotes from this book:

✳ Ratings ✳

Plot: 1 2 3 4 5

Characters:
1 2 3 4 5

Ease of reading:
1 2 3 4 5

Overall
☹ 😐 ☺

74

Title:

Dates
Started: _____
Finished: _____

Source
Bought ○ Loaned ○
From: _____

Author: _____
Publisher: _____   Pub. date _____
Page count: _____
○ Fiction   ○ Non-fiction
  Genre: _____   Subject: _____

My Review:

_____
_____
_____
_____
_____
_____
_____
_____
_____
_____
_____
_____
_____
_____
_____

Inspiration Tree

Why I read it?
_____
⬇
It inspired me to
(read/learn/visit)?
_____
⬇
Who will I
recommend it to?
_____

✳ Ratings ✳

Plot: 1 2 3 4 5
Characters:
1 2 3 4 5
Ease of reading:
1 2 3 4 5
Overall
☹ 😐 ☺

Great quotes from this book:

Paperback ○   Hardback ○   e-book ○   Audiobook ○

Title:

75

Author: _____

Publisher: _____ Pub. date _____

Page count: _____

○ Fiction   ○ Non-fiction

  Genre: _____   Subject: _____

My Review: _____
_____
_____
_____
_____
_____
_____
_____
_____
_____
_____
_____
_____
_____

Great quotes from this book:

Dates
Started: _____
Finished: _____

Source
Bought ○ Loaned ○
From: _____

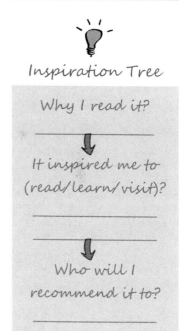

Inspiration Tree

Why I read it?
_____
⬇
It inspired me to
(read/learn/visit)?
_____
_____
⬇
Who will I
recommend it to?
_____

✳ Ratings ✳

Plot: 1 2 3 4 5
Characters:
1 2 3 4 5
Ease of reading:
1 2 3 4 5
Overall
☹ 😐 🙂

76

Title:

Dates
Started: _____
Finished: _____

Source
Bought ○ Loaned ○
From: _____

Author: _____
Publisher: _____ Pub. date _____
Page count: _____
○ Fiction   ○ Non-fiction
  Genre: _____   Subject: _____

💡

Inspiration Tree

Why I read it?
_____
⬇
It inspired me to
(read/learn/visit)?
_____
_____
⬇
Who will I
recommend it to?
_____

My Review:
_____
_____
_____
_____
_____
_____
_____
_____
_____
_____
_____
_____
_____

✳ Ratings ✳
Plot: 1 2 3 4 5
Characters:
1 2 3 4 5
Ease of reading:
1 2 3 4 5
Overall
☹ 😐 ☺

Great quotes from this book:

Paperback ○   Hardback ○   e-book ○   Audiobook ○

Title:

77

Author: _____

Publisher: _____   Pub. date _____

Page count: _____

○ Fiction   ○ Non-fiction

Genre: _____   Subject: _____

Dates
Started: _____
Finished: _____

Source
Bought ○ Loaned ○
From: _____

My Review: _____

_____
_____
_____
_____
_____
_____
_____
_____
_____
_____
_____

Great quotes from this book:

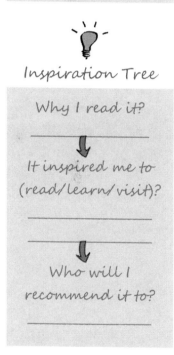

Inspiration Tree

Why I read it?
_____

It inspired me to
(read/learn/visit)?
_____

Who will I
recommend it to?
_____

✳ Ratings ✳

Plot: 1 2 3 4 5
Characters:
1 2 3 4 5
Ease of reading:
1 2 3 4 5
Overall
☹ 😐 🙂

Paperback ○   Hardback ○   e-book ○   Audiobook ○

Title:

Dates
Started: _____
Finished: _____

Source
Bought ○ Loaned ○
From: _____

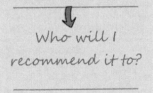

Inspiration Tree

Why I read it?
_____
↓
It inspired me to
(read/learn/visit)?
_____
↓
Who will I
recommend it to?
_____

✳ Ratings ✳

Plot: 1 2 3 4 5
Characters:
1 2 3 4 5
Ease of reading:
1 2 3 4 5
Overall
☹ 😐 ☺

Author: _____
Publisher: _____ Pub. date _____
Page count: _____
○ Fiction   ○ Non-fiction
  Genre: _____   Subject: _____

My Review: _____
_____
_____
_____
_____
_____
_____
_____
_____
_____
_____
_____
_____
_____

Great quotes from this book:

Paperback ○   Hardback ○   e-book ○   Audiobook ○

Title:

79

Author: _____

Publisher: _____   Pub. date _____

Page count: _____

○ Fiction   ○ Non-fiction
  Genre: _____   Subject: _____

My Review: _____
_____
_____
_____
_____
_____
_____
_____
_____
_____
_____
_____
_____
_____

Great quotes from this book:

Dates
Started: _____
Finished: _____

Source
Bought ○   Loaned ○
From: _____

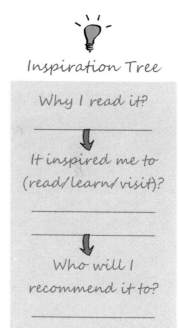

Inspiration Tree

Why I read it?
_____
↓
It inspired me to
(read/learn/visit)?
_____
_____
↓
Who will I
recommend it to?
_____

✳ Ratings ✳

Plot: 1 2 3 4 5
Characters:
1 2 3 4 5
Ease of reading:
1 2 3 4 5
Overall
☹ 😐 ☺

80

Title:

Dates
Started: _____
Finished: _____

Source
Bought ○   Loaned ○
From: _____

💡
Inspiration Tree

Why I read it?
_____
⬇
It inspired me to
(read/learn/visit)?
_____

_____
⬇
Who will I
recommend it to?
_____

✳ Ratings ✳

Plot: 1 2 3 4 5
Characters:
1 2 3 4 5
Ease of reading:
1 2 3 4 5
Overall
☹ 😐 ☺

Author: _____
Publisher: _____   Pub. date _____
Page count: _____
○ Fiction   ○ Non-fiction
  Genre: _____   Subject: _____

My Review:
_____
_____
_____
_____
_____
_____
_____
_____
_____
_____
_____
_____
_____
_____
_____

Great quotes from this book:

Paperback ○   Hardback ○   e-book ○   Audiobook ○

81

Title:

Author: _____

Publisher: _____ Pub. date _____

Page count: _____

○ Fiction   ○ Non-fiction
  Genre: _____   Subject: _____

My Review: _____
_____
_____
_____
_____
_____
_____
_____
_____
_____
_____
_____
_____
_____
_____

Great quotes from this book:

Dates
Started: _____
Finished: _____

Source
Bought ○ Loaned ○
From: _____

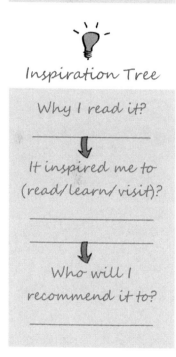

Inspiration Tree

Why I read it?
_____

It inspired me to
(read/learn/visit)?
_____
_____

Who will I
recommend it to?
_____

✕ Ratings ✕

Plot: 1 2 3 4 5
Characters:
1 2 3 4 5
Ease of reading:
1 2 3 4 5
Overall
☹ 😐 ☺

82

Paperback ○   Hardback ○   e-book ○   Audiobook ○

Title:

Dates
Started: _____
Finished: _____

Source
Bought ○   Loaned ○
From: _____

Author: _____
Publisher: _____   Pub. date _____
Page count: _____
○ Fiction   ○ Non-fiction
  Genre: _____   Subject: _____

My Review:

_____

_____

_____

_____

_____

_____

_____

_____

_____

_____

_____

_____

_____

_____

_____

Inspiration Tree

Why I read it?
_____
⬇
It inspired me to
(read/learn/visit)?
_____
⬇
Who will I
recommend it to?
_____

✶ Ratings ✶

Plot: 1 2 3 4 5
Characters:
1 2 3 4 5
Ease of reading:
1 2 3 4 5
Overall
☹ 😐 ☺

Great quotes from this book:

Paperback ○   Hardback ○   e-book ○   Audiobook ○

Title:

83

Author: _____

Publisher: _____   Pub. date _____

Page count: _____

○ Fiction   ○ Non-fiction
   Genre: _____   Subject: _____

Dates
Started: _____
Finished: _____

Source
Bought ○ Loaned ○
From: _____

My Review: _____

_____
_____
_____
_____
_____
_____
_____
_____
_____
_____
_____
_____
_____

Great quotes from this book:

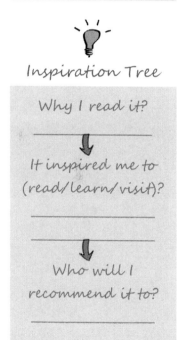

Inspiration Tree

Why I read it?
_____
↓
It inspired me to
(read/learn/visit)?
_____
_____
↓
Who will I
recommend it to?
_____

✳ Ratings ✳

Plot: 1 2 3 4 5
Characters:
1 2 3 4 5
Ease of reading:
1 2 3 4 5
Overall
☹ 😐 ☺

Paperback ○   Hardback ○   e-book ○   Audiobook ○

Title:

Dates
Started: _____
Finished: _____

Source
Bought ○ Loaned ○
From: _____

Inspiration Tree

Why I read it?
_____
↓
It inspired me to
(read/learn/visit)?
_____
_____
↓
Who will I
recommend it to?
_____

✳ Ratings ✳

Plot: 1 2 3 4 5
Characters:
1 2 3 4 5
Ease of reading:
1 2 3 4 5
Overall
☹ 😐 ☺

Author: _____
Publisher: _____   Pub. date _____
Page count: _____
○ Fiction   ○ Non-fiction
  Genre: _____   Subject: _____

My Review: _____
_____
_____
_____
_____
_____
_____
_____
_____
_____
_____
_____
_____

Great quotes from this book:

Paperback ○　　Hardback ○　　e-book ○　　Audiobook ○

85

Title:

Author: _____

Publisher: _____　Pub. date _____

Page count: _____

○ Fiction　　　　　　　　　○ Non-fiction

　Genre: _____　　　Subject: _____

My Review: _____

_____

_____

_____

_____

_____

_____

_____

_____

_____

_____

_____

_____

_____

Great quotes from this book:

Dates
Started: _____
Finished: _____

Source
Bought ○　Loaned ○
From: _____

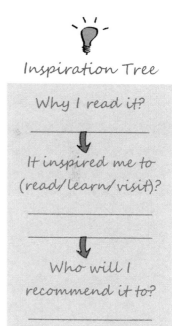

Inspiration Tree

Why I read it?
_____
↓
It inspired me to
(read/learn/visit)?
_____
_____
↓
Who will I
recommend it to?
_____

✳ Ratings ✳

Plot: 1　2　3　4　5
Characters:
1　2　3　4　5
Ease of reading:
1　2　3　4　5
Overall
☹　😐　☺

Paperback ○   Hardback ○   e-book ○   Audiobook ○

Title:

Dates
Started: _____
Finished: _____

Source
Bought ○   Loaned ○
From: _____

Author: _____
Publisher: _____   Pub. date _____
Page count: _____
○ Fiction   ○ Non-fiction
   Genre: _____   Subject: _____

Inspiration Tree

Why I read it?
_____
↓
It inspired me to
(read/learn/visit)?
_____
↓
Who will I
recommend it to?
_____

My Review:
_____
_____
_____
_____
_____
_____
_____
_____
_____
_____
_____
_____
_____

✳ Ratings ✳

Plot: 1 2 3 4 5
Characters:
1 2 3 4 5
Ease of reading:
1 2 3 4 5
Overall
☹ 😐 ☺

Great quotes from this book:

Paperback ○   Hardback ○   e-book ○   Audiobook ○

87

Title:

Author: _____

Publisher: _____   Pub. date _____

Page count: _____

○ Fiction   ○ Non-fiction

Genre: _____   Subject: _____

Dates
Started: _____
Finished: _____

Source
Bought ○ Loaned ○
From: _____

My Review: _____

_____
_____
_____
_____
_____
_____
_____
_____
_____
_____
_____

Inspiration Tree

Why I read it?
_____
↓
It inspired me to
(read/learn/visit)?
_____
↓
Who will I
recommend it to?
_____

Great quotes from this book:

✻ Ratings ✻

Plot: 1 2 3 4 5
Characters:
1 2 3 4 5
Ease of reading:
1 2 3 4 5
Overall
☹ 😐 🙂

Paperback ○   Hardback ○   e-book ○   Audiobook ○

Title:

Dates
Started: _____
Finished: _____

Source
Bought ○ Loaned ○
From: _____

Inspiration Tree

Why I read it?
_____
↓
It inspired me to
(read/learn/visit)?
_____
↓
Who will I
recommend it to?
_____

✳ Ratings ✳

Plot: 1 2 3 4 5
Characters:
1 2 3 4 5
Ease of reading:
1 2 3 4 5
Overall
☹ 😐 ☺

Author: _____
Publisher: _____ Pub. date _____
Page count: _____
○ Fiction   ○ Non-fiction
  Genre: _____   Subject: _____

My Review:
_____
_____
_____
_____
_____
_____
_____
_____
_____
_____
_____
_____
_____
_____
_____

Great quotes from this book:

Paperback ○   Hardback ○   e-book ○   Audiobook ○

89

Title:

Author: _____

Publisher: _____   Pub. date _____

Page count: _____

○ Fiction   ○ Non-fiction

Genre: _____   Subject: _____

Dates
Started: _____
Finished: _____

Source
Bought ○ Loaned ○
From: _____

My Review: _____
_____
_____
_____
_____
_____
_____
_____
_____
_____
_____
_____
_____
_____

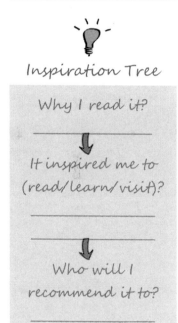

Inspiration Tree

Why I read it?
_____
⬇
It inspired me to
(read/learn/visit)?
_____
_____
⬇
Who will I
recommend it to?
_____

✳ Ratings ✳

Plot: 1 2 3 4 5
Characters:
1 2 3 4 5
Ease of reading:
1 2 3 4 5
Overall
☹ 😐 ☺

Great quotes from this book:

90

Title:

Dates
Started: _____
Finished: _____

Source
Bought ○ Loaned ○
From: _____

Author: _____

Publisher: _____   Pub. date _____

Page count: _____

○ Fiction   ○ Non-fiction

  Genre: _____   Subject: _____

Inspiration Tree

Why I read it?
_____
⬇
It inspired me to
(read/learn/visit)?
_____
_____
⬇
Who will I
recommend it to?
_____

My Review:

_____
_____
_____
_____
_____
_____
_____
_____
_____
_____
_____
_____
_____
_____

�֍ Ratings ✲

Plot: 1 2 3 4 5
Characters:
1 2 3 4 5
Ease of reading:
1 2 3 4 5
Overall
☹ 😐 ☺

Great quotes from this book:

Paperback ○   Hardback ○   e-book ○   Audiobook ○

91

Title:

Author: _____

Publisher: _____ Pub. date _____

Page count: _____

○ Fiction   ○ Non-fiction

   Genre: _____   Subject. _____

Dates
Started: _____
Finished: _____

Source
Bought ○   Loaned ○
From: _____

My Review: _____

_____
_____
_____
_____
_____
_____
_____
_____
_____
_____
_____
_____

Inspiration Tree

Why I read it?
_____

⬇

It inspired me to
(read/learn/visit)?
_____
_____

⬇

Who will I
recommend it to?
_____

Great quotes from this book.

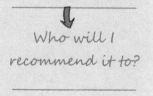

✳ Ratings ✳

Plot. 1 2 3 4 5
Characters.
1 2 3 4 5
Ease of reading:
1 2 3 4 5
Overall
☹ 😐 🙂

Paperback ○   Hardback ○   e-book ○   Audiobook ○

Title:

Dates
Started: _____
Finished: _____

Source
Bought ○   Loaned ○
From: _____

Author: _____
Publisher: _____   Pub. date _____
Page count: _____
○ Fiction   ○ Non-fiction
   Genre: _____   Subject: _____

My Review: _____
_____
_____
_____
_____
_____
_____
_____
_____
_____
_____
_____
_____
_____
_____
_____
_____

Inspiration Tree

Why I read it?
_____
↓
It inspired me to
(read/learn/visit)?
_____
_____
↓
Who will I
recommend it to?
_____

✳ Ratings ✳

Plot: 1 2 3 4 5
Characters:
1 2 3 4 5
Ease of reading:
1 2 3 4 5
Overall
☹ 😐 ☺

Great quotes from this book:

Paperback ○   Hardback ○   e-book ○   Audiobook ○

93

Title:

Author: _____

Publisher: _____   Pub. date _____

Page count: _____

○ Fiction   ○ Non-fiction

Genre: _____   Subject: _____

Dates
Started: _____
Finished: _____

Source
Bought ○   Loaned ○
From: _____

My Review: _____

_____
_____
_____
_____
_____
_____
_____
_____
_____
_____
_____
_____
_____
_____

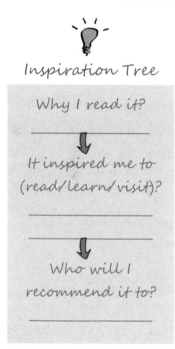

Inspiration Tree

Why I read it?
_____
⬇
It inspired me to
(read/learn/visit)?
_____
⬇
Who will I
recommend it to?
_____

✳ Ratings ✳

Plot: 1 2 3 4 5
Characters:
1 2 3 4 5
Ease of reading:
1 2 3 4 5
Overall
☹ 😐 ☺

Great quotes from this book:

Paperback ○   Hardback ○   e-book ○   Audiobook ○

Title:

Author: _____

Publisher: _____   Pub. date _____

Page count: _____

○ Fiction   ○ Non-fiction

Genre: _____   Subject: _____

Dates

Started: _____

Finished: _____

Source

Bought ○   Loaned ○

From: _____

Inspiration Tree

Why I read it?

_____

⬇

It inspired me to
(read/learn/visit)?

_____

_____

⬇

Who will I
recommend it to?

_____

✳ Ratings ✳

Plot: 1 2 3 4 5

Characters:
1 2 3 4 5

Ease of reading:
1 2 3 4 5

Overall

☹ 😐 🙂

My Review: _____

_____

_____

_____

_____

_____

_____

_____

_____

_____

_____

_____

_____

_____

_____

Great quotes from this book:

Paperback ○   Hardback ○   e-book ○   Audiobook ○

95

Title:

Author: _____

Publisher: _____ Pub. date _____

Page count: _____

○ Fiction   ○ Non-fiction

   Genre: _____   Subject: _____

Dates
Started: _____
Finished: _____

Source
Bought ○ Loaned ○
From: _____

My Review:

_____
_____
_____
_____
_____
_____
_____
_____
_____
_____
_____
_____
_____
_____
_____

Great quotes from this book:

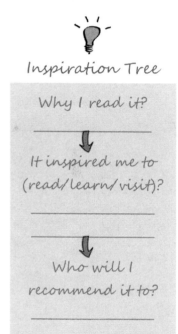

Inspiration Tree

Why I read it?
_____
↓
It inspired me to
(read/learn/visit)?
_____
_____
↓
Who will I
recommend it to?
_____

✷ Ratings ✷

Plot: 1 2 3 4 5
Characters:
1 2 3 4 5
Ease of reading:
1 2 3 4 5
Overall
☹ 😐 ☺

Paperback ○   Hardback ○   e-book ○   Audiobook ○

Title:

Dates
Started: _____
Finished: _____

Source
Bought ○   Loaned ○
From: _____

Author: _____
Publisher: _____   Pub. date _____
Page count: _____
○ Fiction   ○ Non-fiction
   Genre: _____   Subject: _____

My Review: _____
_____
_____
_____
_____
_____
_____
_____
_____
_____
_____
_____
_____
_____
_____

Inspiration Tree

Why I read it?
_____
⬇
It inspired me to
(read/learn/visit)?
_____
⬇
Who will I
recommend it to?
_____

✳ Ratings ✳

Plot: 1 2 3 4 5
Characters:
1 2 3 4 5
Ease of reading:
1 2 3 4 5
Overall
☹ 😐 ☺

Great quotes from this book:

Paperback ○   Hardback ○   e-book ○   Audiobook ○

Title:

97

Author: _____

Publisher: _____ Pub. date _____

Page count: _____

○ Fiction   ○ Non-fiction
   Genre: _____   Subject: _____

Source
Bought ○   Loaned ○
From: _____

My Review: _____

_____

_____

_____

_____

_____

_____

_____

_____

_____

_____

_____

_____

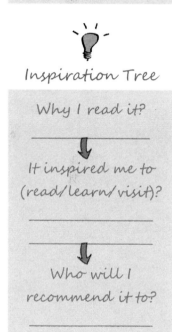

Inspiration Tree

Why I read it?
_____
⬇
It inspired me to
(read/learn/visit)?
_____
_____
⬇
Who will I
recommend it to?
_____

✳ Ratings ✳

Plot: 1 2 3 4 5
Characters:
1 2 3 4 5
Ease of reading:
1 2 3 4 5

Overall
☹ 😐 ☺

Great quotes from this book:

98

Title:

Dates
Started: _____
Finished: _____

Source
Bought ○ Loaned ○
From: _____

Author: _____

Publisher: _____   Pub. date _____

Page count: _____

○ Fiction   ○ Non-fiction
  Genre: _____   Subject: _____

Inspiration Tree

Why I read it?
_____
⬇
It inspired me to
(read/learn/visit)?
_____
⬇
Who will I
recommend it to?
_____

My Review: _____

_____
_____
_____
_____
_____
_____
_____
_____
_____
_____
_____
_____
_____
_____

✳ Ratings ✳

Plot: 1 2 3 4 5
Characters:
1 2 3 4 5
Ease of reading:
1 2 3 4 5
Overall
☹ 😐 ☺

Great quotes from this book:

Paperback ○   Hardback ○   e-book ○   Audiobook ○

Title:

99

Author: _____

Publisher: _____   Pub. date _____

Page count: _____

○ Fiction   ○ Non-fiction

  Genre: _____   Subject: _____

Dates
Started: _____
Finished: _____

Source
Bought ○   Loaned ○
From: _____

My Review: _____

_____

_____

_____

_____

_____

_____

_____

_____

_____

_____

_____

_____

_____

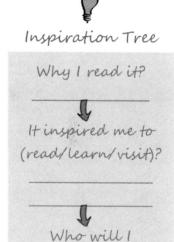

Inspiration Tree

Why I read it?
_____
↓
It inspired me to
(read/learn/visit)?
_____
_____
↓
Who will I
recommend it to?
_____

✳ Ratings ✳

Plot: 1 2 3 4 5
Characters:
1 2 3 4 5
Ease of reading:
1 2 3 4 5
Overall
☹ 😐 ☺

Great quotes from this book:

100

Title:

Dates
Started: _____
Finished: _____

Source
Bought ○ Loaned ○
From: _____

Author: _____
Publisher: _____   Pub. date _____
Page count: _____
○ Fiction   ○ Non-fiction
  Genre: _____   Subject: _____

My Review: _____
_____
_____
_____
_____
_____
_____
_____
_____
_____
_____
_____
_____
_____
_____
_____

Inspiration Tree

Why I read it?
_____
↓
It inspired me to
(read/learn/visit)?
_____
↓
Who will I
recommend it to?
_____

✳ Ratings ✳

Plot: 1 2 3 4 5
Characters:
1 2 3 4 5
Ease of reading:
1 2 3 4 5
Overall
☹ 😐 🙂

Great quotes from this book:

The Big Read

Top 100 Voted Fiction Books

- 1. The Lord of the Rings, JRR Tolkien
- 2. Pride and Prejudice, Jane Austen
- 3. His Dark Materials, Philip Pullman
- 4. The Hitchhiker's Guide to the Galaxy, Douglas Adams
- 5. Harry Potter and the Goblet of Fire, JK Rowling
- 6. To Kill a Mockingbird, Harper Lee
- 7. Winnie the Pooh, AA Milne
- 8. Nineteen Eighty-Four, George Orwell
- 9. The Lion, the Witch and the Wardrobe, CS Lewis
- 10. Jane Eyre, Charlotte Brontë
- 11. Catch-22, Joseph Heller
- 12. Wuthering Heights, Emily Brontë
- 13. Birdsong, Sebastian Faulks
- 14. Rebecca, Daphne du Maurier
- 15. The Catcher in the Rye, JD Salinger
- 16. The Wind in the Willows, Kenneth Grahame
- 17. Great Expectations, Charles Dickens
- 18. Little Women, Louisa May Alcott
- 19. Captain Corelli's Mandolin, Louis de Bernieres
- 20. War and Peace, Leo Tolstoy
- 21. Gone with the Wind, Margaret Mitchell
- 22. Harry Potter And The Philosopher's Stone, JK Rowling
- 23. Harry Potter And The Chamber Of Secrets, JK Rowling
- 24. Harry Potter And The Prisoner Of Azkaban, JK Rowling
- 25. The Hobbit, JRR Tolkien
- 26. Tess Of The D'Urbervilles, Thomas Hardy
- 27. Middlemarch, George Eliot
- 28. A Prayer For Owen Meany, John Irving
- 29. The Grapes Of Wrath, John Steinbeck
- 30. Alice's Adventures In Wonderland, Lewis Carroll

- 31. The Story Of Tracy Beaker, Jacqueline Wilson
- 32. One Hundred Years Of Solitude, Gabriel García Márquez
- 33. The Pillars Of The Earth, Ken Follett
- 34. David Copperfield, Charles Dickens
- 35. Charlie And The Chocolate Factory, Roald Dahl
- 36. Treasure Island, Robert Louis Stevenson
- 37. A Town Like Alice, Nevil Shute
- 38. Persuasion, Jane Austen
- 39. Dune, Frank Herbert
- 40. Emma, Jane Austen
- 41. Anne Of Green Gables, LM Montgomery
- 42. Watership Down, Richard Adams
- 43. The Great Gatsby, F Scott Fitzgerald
- 44. The Count Of Monte Cristo, Alexandre Dumas
- 45. Brideshead Revisited, Evelyn Waugh
- 46. Animal Farm, George Orwell
- 47. A Christmas Carol, Charles Dickens
- 48. Far From The Madding Crowd, Thomas Hardy
- 49. Goodnight Mister Tom, Michelle Magorian
- 50. The Shell Seekers, Rosamunde Pilc
- 51. The Secret Garden, Frances Hodgson Burnett
- 52. Of Mice And Men, John Steinbeck
- 53. The Stand, Stephen King
- 54. Anna Karenina, Leo Tolstoy
- 55. A Suitable Boy, Vikram Seth
- 56. The BFG, Roald Dahl
- 57. Swallows And Amazons, Arthur Ransome
- 58. Black Beauty, Anna Sewell
- 59. Artemis Fowl, Eoin Colfer
- 60. Crime And Punishment, Fyodor Dostoyevsky
- 61. Noughts And Crosses, Malorie Blackman
- 62. Memoirs Of A Geisha, Arthur Golden
- 63. A Tale Of Two Cities, Charles Dickens
- 64. The Thorn Birds, Colleen McCollough
- 65. Mort, Terry Pratchett

- 66. The Magic Faraway Tree, Enid Blyton
- 67. The Magus, John Fowles
- 68. Good Omens, Terry Pratchett and Neil Gaiman
- 69. Guards! Guards!, Terry Pratchett
- 70. Lord Of The Flies, William Golding
- 71. Perfume, Patrick Süskind
- 72. The Ragged Trousered Philanthropists, Robert Tressell
- 73. Night Watch, Terry Pratchett
- 74. Matilda, Roald Dahl
- 75. Bridget Jones's Diary, Helen Fielding
- 76. The Secret History, Donna Tartt
- 77. The Woman In White, Wilkie Collins
- 78. Ulysses, James Joyce
- 79. Bleak House, Charles Dickens
- 80. Double Act, Jacqueline Wilson
- 81. The Twits, Roald Dahl
- 82. I Capture The Castle, Dodie Smith
- 83. Holes, Louis Sachar
- 84. Gormenghast, Mervyn Peake
- 85. The God Of Small Things, Arundhati Roy
- 86. Vicky Angel, Jacqueline Wilson
- 87. Brave New World, Aldous Huxley
- 88. Cold Comfort Farm, Stella Gibbons
- 89. Magician, Raymond E Feist
- 90. On The Road, Jack Kerouac
- 91. The Godfather, Mario Puzo
- 92. The Clan Of The Cave Bear, Jean M Auel
- 93. The Colour Of Magic, Terry Pratchett
- 94. The Alchemist, Paulo Coelho
- 95. Katherine, Anya Seton
- 96. Kane And Abel, Jeffrey Archer
- 97. Love In The Time Of Cholera, Gabriel García Márquez
- 98. Girls In Love, Jacqueline Wilson
- 99. The Princess Diaries, Meg Cabot
- 100. Midnight's Children, Salman Rushdie

Notes: (books to read, new authors, book supplier's contact details, reading resources etc.)

Loan Record

Book	Borrowed from	Leant to	Date Borrowed	Date Returned